Fatherhood
in 60 Minutes or Less

101 Humorous Observations,
Rules of Thumb, and Untold Truths
for Fathers by any Definition

Mark M. Welfley

FATHERHOOD IN 60 MINUTES OR LESS: 101 HUMOROUS OBSERVATIONS,
RULES OF THUMB AND UNTOLD TRUTHS FOR FATHERS BY ANY DEFINITION

Copyright © 2019 Atlantic Publishing Group, Inc.

1405 SW 6th Avenue • Ocala, Florida 34471 • Phone 352-622-1825 • Fax 352-622-1875
Website: www.atlantic-pub.com • Email: sales@atlantic-pub.com
SAN Number: 268-1250

Library of Congress Cataloging-in-Publication Data

Names: Welfley, Mark, author.
Title: Fatherhood in 60 minutes or less : 101 humorous observations, rules of thumb and
    untold truths / by Mark Welfley.
Other titles: Fatherhood in sixty minutes or less
Description: Ocala : Atlantic Publishing Group, Inc., [2019]
Identifiers: LCCN 2019016974 (print) | LCCN 2019018187 (ebook) | ISBN
    9781620236444 (ebook) | ISBN 1620236443 (ebook) | ISBN 9781620236437
    (alk. paper) ISBN 1620236435 (alk. paper)
Subjects: LCSH: Fatherhood—Humor. | Parenting—Humor.
Classification: LCC HQ756 (ebook) | LCC HQ756 .W435 2019 (print) | DDC
    306.874/2—dc23
LC record available at https://lccn.loc.gov/2019016974

Printed in the United States

PROJECT MANAGER: Danielle Lieneman
INTERIOR LAYOUT AND JACKET DESIGN: Nicole Sturk

Table of Contents

Introduction..1

Behavior 3

Conversation 21

Dress Code...37

Eats 41

The Father Code...53

Health...63

Home..71

Memories 75

Ouch..83

Pets 87

Play 91

Time Together...109

Travel 115

Acknowledgments 121

About the Author..123

– Introduction –

You can learn a lot from your children. I became a father for the first time at the age of 47 with the birth of my daughter, Kat. She and my son, Christian, have taught me much about myself, just as I have learned much about them. I have also learned that there is a lot that books on fatherhood cannot teach you. This book fills in some of the gaps with observations, rules of thumb, and untold truths that I wish I had known and now use regularly.

Behavior

— 1 —

Children will accept instruction from anyone so long as "anyone" is not their parent.

—2—

Ask your children to
perform one act of kindness
per day. You start first.

3

The biggest behavior changes in a child are usually from fatigue, boredom, hunger, and sugar (and sometimes siblings).

— 4 —

Children will remember
what you think they won't.
What they do remember
will be different from what
you expect.

–5–

Teaching children is the art
of repetition with a different
explanation each time.

— 6 —

The measure of a child
is his/her response to
something he/she does not
want to do. The measure of
a father is his response to his
child when this happens.

7

The most effective way to change a child's behavior is by taking away or limiting access to something that the child values.

— 8 —

Hurrying a child always
has consequences.

— 9 —

Teaching a child is like
shaking an elephant's tail:
Eventually the trunk will
move, but you just don't
know when.

—10—

Don't say don't. Children hear every word except don't and then behave accordingly. Instead of saying "Don't Run," say "Please Walk." (I learned this from my sister.)

— 11 —

You can manage, supervise, and guide children, but you cannot control them.

12

Young children speak
with their behavior;
older children speak with
their voice.

— 13 —

The younger the child, the more he/she is angry at a situation rather than a specific person. Don't take his/her anger personally.

—14—

When you discipline your children, you are often disciplining yourself.

— 15 —

The only time I raise my voice to my children is when they don't listen or hurt someone … or I am cheering them on in an activity.

16

Learning the rules
of behavior is more
important to a child than
breaking them.

— 17 —

When the training wheels come off, the real training begins.

Conversation

— 18 —

The way to a child's heart is
through humor, not holler.

— 19 —

Giving answers to children
is convenient, but letting
them discover the answers
by themselves takes more
patience from everyone.

—20—

Honest compliments and
honest criticism matter
to a child.

21

Eye contact can speak
volumes.

.

— 22 —

Apologize to your child if
you are wrong.

—23—

If you say "just a minute" each time your child asks you for something, your child will learn to do the same to you.

— 24 —

Answer a question with a
question when you can.

25

"Because I said I would" is a very powerful statement to a child. A child knows when a promise has been kept.

— 26 —

The three greatest words a father can hear are "I love you," but the two most endearing words are "Oh, Daaad."

— 27 —

A child's attention span
for spoken words is about
twice as many sentences as
his/her age.

—28—

You learn less from your children by asking questions and more from your children by being present to them during their quietest moments.

—29—

The Substitution Principle:
If you cannot attend to your
child's request promptly,
offer something equivalent
at a later time. Then, deliver
on your promise.

—30—

Tell stories from your past to illustrate your points and read stories that are true to teach your child about history.

— 31 —

If you want a refreshing
perspective, ask a child
to answer a question to
which you do not know
the answer.

— 32 —

Tomorrow is like a lifetime
away to a child.

Dress Code

— 33 —

When your children put their shoes on the wrong feet, it is a humorous step forward.

—34—

When you venture out with your children, remember to wear clothes with pockets. You will need to find places to put your phone, your children's necessities, and a few other things that you will pick up along the way. My children told me that cargo pants are not cool anymore, but they work well.

— 35 —

Allowing a child to dress themselves appropriate to weather and occasion but not to style shows self-confidence on the part of both father and child.

Eats

—36—

Add bacon to nearly any meal
to make it more palatable
to a child.

— 37 —

Never serve children a meal
portion that is more than
you can eat because you
might wind up finishing
their meal for them.

—38—

If children were around before peanut butter and jelly and grilled cheese were invented, what did they eat?

—39—

Serve desserts in smaller bowls and use smaller spoons. It looks like more.

—40—

A child hungry for more
dessert did not eat enough
dinner.

— 41 —

Baked into a child's DNA
is the refusal to eat the crust
of a piece of bread.

42

It's easier to put ice cream into an ice cream cone with a fork versus a spoon.

43

The more difficult the fruit or vegetable is to pronounce, the more likely it is the child will not eat it — with the exception of peas.

— 44 —

If you don't tell children what they are eating, they will probably like it.

45

The amount of ice cream that you serve your child should be equal to the size of his/her fist. The serving size of a candy bar should be equal to the length of your child's middle finger.

—46—

The rite of passage from younger child to older child is the ability to eat an ice cream cone without runs, drips, and sticky hands. The rite of passage to fatherhood is the ability to use super-strength clear glue without getting your fingers stuck together.

The Father
Code

— 47 —

Your fatherly instincts
are almost always right.
Trust them.

—48—

A child's biggest confidence builder is a skill, talent, or ability that he/she can call his/her own.

— 49 —

When you reach your last
measure of patience, reach
for a little more.

—50—

Smile at your children unless you are unhappy with them.

—51—

The best way to get an idea
through to your child is
by example.

— 52 —

Be present to your children,
especially when you think
they are not watching. They
are always watching.

—53—

Parent with your heart.
Teach with your head.

— 54 —

Fatherhood is constant
awareness.

—55—

Overpay your children's caretakers. You can never have too many quality people available to care for your most precious assets.

Health

–56–

When you care for children, you have choices: work, sleep or hygiene. Most days, you can pick any two.

—57—

You can teach your children not to become too predictable by asking them to brush their teeth and eat their meals with their opposite hand.

-58-

The legitimate reasons for a child to stay home from school are vomiting and/or a fever — unless a sufficient argument is made for another affliction.

—59—

If you want to know the height of your child, don't go to a doctor; go to an amusement park. They measure to the last hair.

60

Ask your children to brush only the teeth they are interested in keeping and wash only where they have skin.

-61-

The third greatest gift you can give to your child is your commitment to his/her good health. This gift will last a lifetime. (Your love and your time are first and second.)

62

You cannot take care of your
children unless you take
care of yourself.

Home

—63—

No matter how large your home or family size, you will never seem to have enough space.

64

Houses with complete circles inside them are more fun for children (and more dangerous).

Memories

—65—

You will remember your child's first birthday the most. Your child will remember it the least.

—66—

The big picture of your child's life is a prism of small windows.

— 67 —

You won't forget or underappreciate the hugs your children give you.

—68—

The nights with children can be long, but the years are short.

— 69 —

Wishing away the days
may have you wishing for
them back.

—70—

Your children will
appreciate the music of your
generation, if you make the
time to play it for them.

—71—

Short thank you notes
from children are long
remembered.

Ouch

72

An accidental bump from your child's head under your chin hurts more than you think, so grab your child's head before kissing him/her.

— 73 —

The first thing a child says
to another who is injured
is not "Are you OK?" but
"Can I see it" (the wound)?

Pets

—74—

Your child will walk your
new pet exactly the number
of times he/she asked for
the new pet.

—75—

Dogs love to pee in leaves.
Children love to play
in leaves.

—76—

A dog always gives
100 percent and never
complains, which makes
a dog a role model
for children.

Play

— 77 —

The longer it takes children to establish the rules for a game, the shorter the game will last.

78

Keep a few Lego® sets hidden in your home for when your children are bored. They also work well as emergency gifts.

—79—

A large, wide-open parking lot is the best place to learn how to ride a bicycle.

—80—

Learning to swim is
invaluable to a child and
emancipating to a parent.

-81-

The difference between an old father and a young one is measured by how many rides the father goes on with his children at an amusement park.

— 82 —

If you can't go to an
amusement park, try a car
wash. It's like a water thrill
ride to young children.

83

Tree houses are fun to a child for 15 minutes.

— 84 —

Take your children to a
different park or playground
each week and then
rank them.

-85-

Children have the energy to play endlessly. However, when you ask for their help, they will ask for a break every 10 minutes.

—86—

Adjusting poor-quality swimming goggles wastes as much time as a child will spend playing in the pool.

— 87 —

Children have the most
fun 10 minutes before you
have to leave.

88

A water battle with small plastic cups and a few water buckets is more fun — and less cleanup — than a water balloon fight.

—89—

Slightly deflate the tires on your child's starter bike to improve leg strength, perfect balance, and reduce speed.

—90—

A committed father takes off his shoes and plays with his children at the beach.

— 91 —

If you want to teach your child how to add two numbers that equal 10, go bowling.

—92—

How a child transitions
from one activity to another
is almost as important as
the activity itself.

Time Together

93

If you don't know what to do with your children, take them out for ice cream.

—94—

Focus on what you have,
not what you don't.

95

When you play with your
children, turn off your
technology and turn on
your mind.

—96—

If you are not sure what to
do with a despondent child,
start by leaving him/her
alone for as many minutes
as he/she is old.

97

When you are out and
about, leave for home when
your children are still in a
good mood.

Travel

98

The best vacation
entertainment for children is
a swimming pool.

99

A good vacation can undo
many of your children's
good habits, but it's
worth it.

– 100 –

A survival kit for an infant consists of wipes, diapers, Cheerios®, and a pacifier. A survival kit for a child requires tissues, Band-Aids®, and snacks.

— 101 —

Wake up your children
last when leaving on an
early morning trip to best
economize your time.

– Acknowledgments –

It takes a village and its pets to publish a book. My wife, Allison, proved an excellent sounding board and keeper of the book's focus. My children, Kat and Christian, have lived their lives unknowingly in a Petri dish. Without them, this book is not possible. Thanks to my parents and siblings for evaluating the content of this book and offering their own observations, rules of thumb, and untold truths. I enjoyed our conversations. Lastly, thanks to our dog, Max. Our walks have allowed for reflection, brainstorming, wordsmithing, and a freeing up of the creative process.

– About the Author –

Mark M. Welfley is an assistant professor of practice at the University of Akron. He is a published author and awarded professor in the area of ethics. Welfley owns a small IT firm, is a guest speaker at numerous organizations, and can be heard regularly talking tech and fatherhood on a local radio program. He holds an MBA from California State University at Dominguez Hills and is an ever-mindful married father of two young children. Connect with Mark and learn more about fatherhood at fathers101.com